AR PTS: 1.0

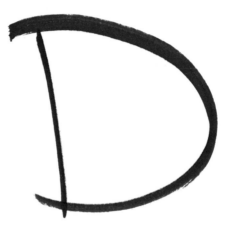

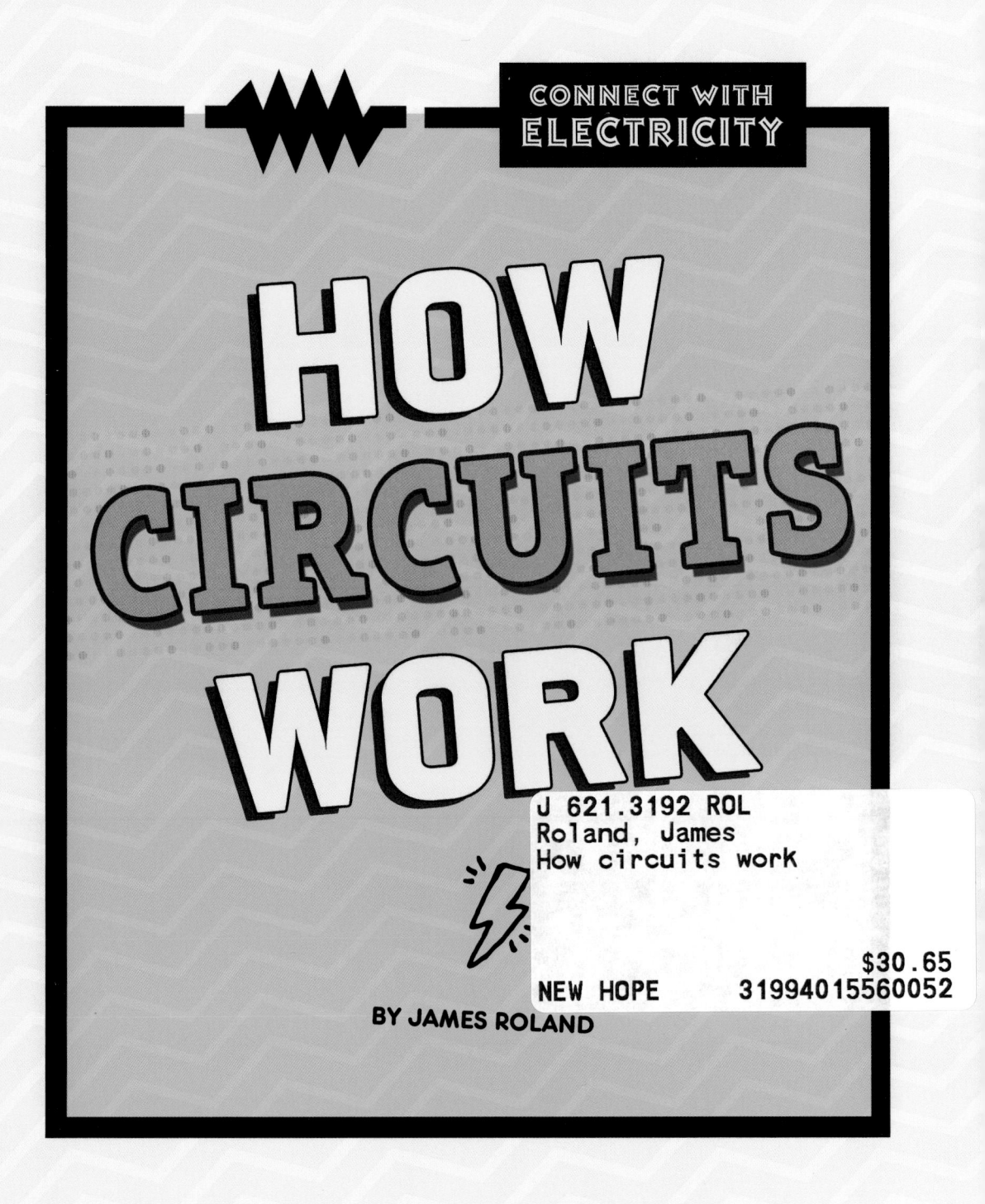

CONNECT WITH ELECTRICITY

HOW CIRCUITS WORK

BY JAMES ROLAND

LERNER PUBLICATIONS ◆ MINNEAPOLIS

To Heidi, Christopher, Alexa, and
Carson . . . you complete me.
—J.R.

Special thanks to content consultant Neal Clements, Adjunct Professor of
Electrical and Computer Engineering, North Dakota State University

Lerner Publications Company
A division of Lerner Publishing Group, Inc.
241 First Avenue North
Minneapolis, MN USA 55401

For reading levels and more information, look up this title at
www.lernerbooks.com.

Main body text set in Aptifer Slab LT Pro 12/18.
Typeface provided by Linotype AG.

Library of Congress Cataloging-in-Publication Data

Names: Roland, James, author.
Title: How circuits work / by James Roland.
Description: Minneapolis : Lerner Publications, [2017] | Series: Connect with
    electricity | Audience: Ages 8–11. | Audience: Grades 4 to 6. | Includes
    bibliographical references and index.
Identifiers: LCCN 2015044352 (print) | LCCN 2015046013 (ebook) |
    ISBN 9781512407785 (lb : alk. paper) | ISBN 9781512410075 (eb pdf)
Subjects: LCSH: Electric circuits—Juvenile literature. | Electric networks—
    Juvenile literature. | Electricity—Juvenile literature.
Classification: LCC TK148 .R627 2017 (print) | LCC TK148 (ebook) | DDC
    621.319/2—dc23

LC record available at http://lccn.loc.gov/2015044352

Manufactured in the United States of America
1-39350-21162-4/1/2016

CONTENTS

NASA astronauts Scott Kelly *(top)* and Terry Virts *(bottom)* are working in the Destiny Laboratory of the International Space Station (ISS). The circuits that provide power to the ISS allow astronauts to live and work in space.

A lightning storm is crackling outside when suddenly the lights go out. Out the window, you see that other homes on your street are also without power. Eventually the lights come back on. You find out later that a bolt of lightning struck some of the equipment that supplies electricity to your neighborhood. To restore the electricity, the power company had to repair the large electrical circuit that provides energy to the homes on your street and others nearby.

A circuit is a path that electric current travels to provide energy to lights, cities, or anything that needs electricity to work. A circuit is a closed path—it begins and ends in the same place without a break anywhere along the way. During the lightning storm, that closed path opened up—the electric current was stopped, at least for a little while.

Circuits are at the heart of all electronics. Without them, we wouldn't be able to power computers, speakers, the electric lights in your home, or even the International Space Station. To really understand how electricity is used all around you, you need to know your circuits.

CHAPTER ONE

CIRCUITS GET ELECTRICITY MOVING

When you turn on a flashlight, it might seem as if electrical energy flows from the batteries to the lightbulb and that's the end of it. But to actually get electricity moving, you need a circuit—a path in which the electric current runs through a power source like a battery and through components like a lightbulb.

An electric current is the movement of electrons through a conductor like copper wire. Electrons are negatively charged particles that are too small to see. An electron is one of three parts of an atom, the tiny units of matter that make up everything in the universe. Electrons orbit, or circle, the atom's nucleus. That nucleus is made up of protons, or positively charged particles, and neutrons, which have no charge. Electrons are attracted to the positive charge of the protons, so they spin around the nucleus very fast.

It's that movement of countless electrons through a circuit that keeps

The circuits providing power to your TV let you play video games!

your video games working and your refrigerator running. In a circuit, the electrons carry the electric charge. The current is simply the flow of an electric charge.

Circuits are designed to do very specific jobs. Your flashlight contains a small circuit—one that you could design and build yourself. But the circuits that provide power to your whole town are huge and require teams of engineers and electricians to keep running.

Whether they're made up of a few parts or a few million parts, all electrical circuits are based on the same concept. They need three basic things: a power source, a conducting path, and a load.

A power source is where the energy comes from. It can be a battery you hold in your hand or a giant power plant that runs on solar energy or natural gas. A conducting path is a substance the electrons move through. Copper wire is a commonly used conductor. Electrons can also move easily through aluminum, but not as well as they can travel through copper or silver. The last key ingredient of any circuit is the load. The load is the object

DIAGRAM OF A CIRCUIT

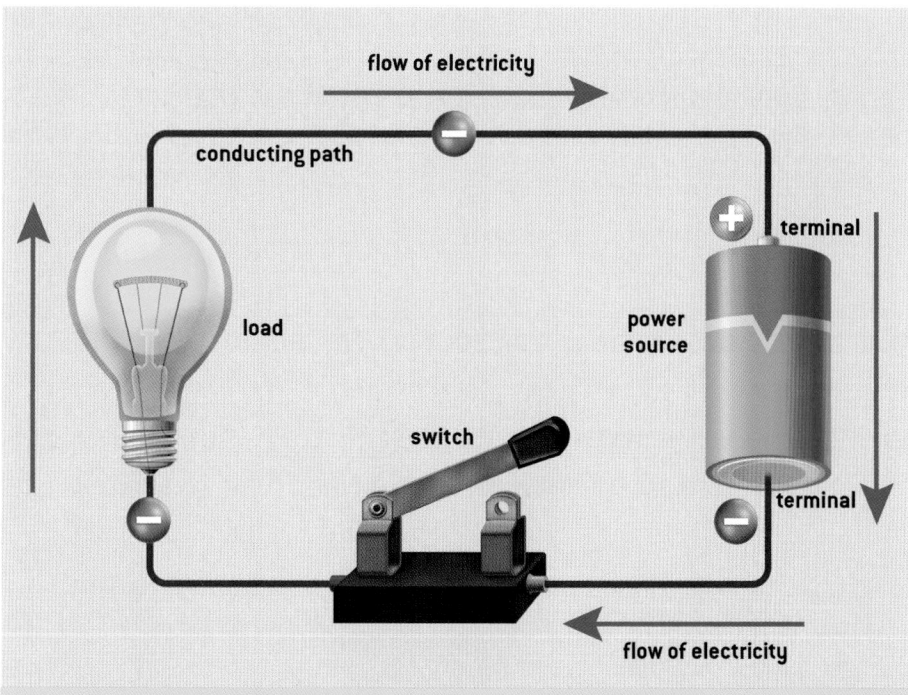

The switch in this circuit is open, meaning the electrons cannot travel through the complete circuit, so the lightbulb will not light.

you're trying to power. It's the item or items that will consume the electrical energy. A load could be a television or an electric guitar or the lights in your school cafeteria.

One end of the conducting path will be attached to the positive terminal of the power source. Terminals are what connect a battery to the rest of a circuit. The positive terminal has a positive charge, which attracts electrons. On a battery, it's the end with the plus sign. The other end of the conducting path is attached to the negative terminal on the battery, marked with a minus sign. The negative terminal has a negative charge, which repels electrons. When a circuit is created, the electrons are drawn toward the positive end and pushed from the negative end. That's what gets them flowing through the circuit.

The conducting path—usually wire—also runs through the load. The load takes the energy it needs and lets the rest of the unused electrons keep going. The electrons move along the conducting path through the power source from the negative end to the positive end because they're attracted to positively charged particles.

These batteries have a positive terminal on one end and a negative terminal on the opposite end. Some batteries look different, but they all have the same basic parts.

BEN FRANKLIN, FOUNDER OF BATTERIES

You may know Benjamin Franklin as one of the founders of the United States. But did you know he was also fascinated with electricity? Through his many experiments, he invented and named the first electrical battery. He didn't know about positively and negatively charged particles, so he just called the moving particles in the battery "charge." Modern scientists and engineers know those particles are negatively charged electrons that move from the negative end of a battery, through a circuit, to the positive end.

This movement of the electrons is the current. It will keep flowing until something interrupts it. Usually that's a switch that blocks the flow of electric current somewhere along the conducting path.

CONTROLLING THE CURRENT

We know how an electric current moves through a circuit, but what is it that gets the current going in the first place? And how do you measure the force that moves electrons along the conducting path? These are both questions that engineers and electricians must be able to answer before they can design complex circuits.

The force that gets electrons moving is called voltage. You've probably heard the term *volt*, as in a 9-volt battery. A volt is a unit of measurement, like an inch or a liter. It measures electrical pressure, or how much force is being applied to make the electrons move.

Another way to think about volts is that they represent the difference in potential energy from one part of a circuit to another. Potential energy is stored energy. Picture an archer with a bow and arrow. When he pulls back on the bowstring, he creates a lot of stored energy that is ready to be released.

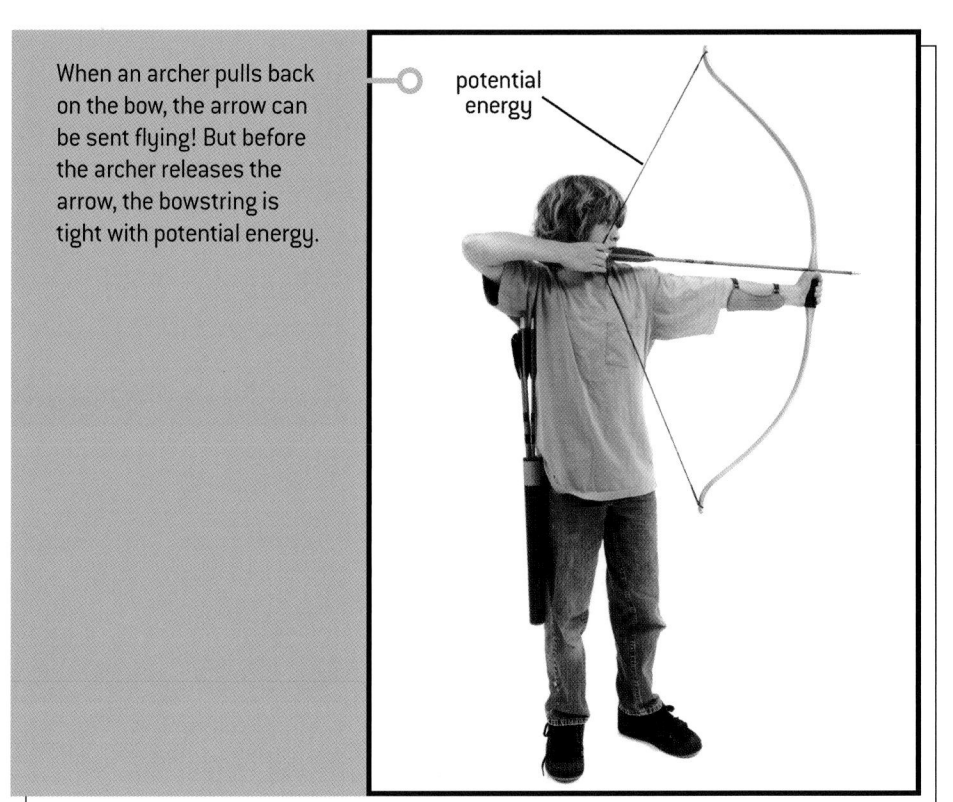

When an archer pulls back on the bow, the arrow can be sent flying! But before the archer releases the arrow, the bowstring is tight with potential energy.

potential energy

A battery provides the energy in this remote controller to send signals to the car, setting it in motion.

It's the same for a battery. The voltage is the potential energy difference between the negative and positive ends of the battery when it's hooked up to a circuit. In a circuit, one point will always have more charge than another point. That difference is voltage.

The potential energy stays inside a battery until the battery is connected to a circuit. Once the positive and negative terminals of a 9-volt battery are connected by a circuit, 9 volts of electric pressure move through the circuit.

To complete a circuit, the conducting path must connect both terminals of the power source. Once that connection is made, electrons start moving from the negative terminal through the rest of the circuit to the positive terminal.

The way we measure the flow of electrons in a circuit is with amperes, or amps for short. Like a volt, an amp is a unit of measure. It measures the amount of electricity running through a wire or other conductor.

WHO WAS OHM, AND HOW DID HE GET HIS OWN LAW?

Ohm's law is one of the most useful equations in electronics, and it is vital to the design of a well-working circuit. It's named after Georg Ohm (1789–1854), a German math teacher and scientist. Ohm (right) liked to experiment with electronics. He was able to show how resistance increased as the length of the wire in a circuit increased because more electron collisions will occur in a long wire than a short wire. We call a unit of resistance an ohm (written as Ω) in his honor.

Another important measurement in a circuit is resistance. It's measured in ohms. Resistance measures how much difficulty the electrons face as they race along the conducting path. The greater the resistance in a wire, the more likely the electrons are to bump into one another along the way. For your circuit to operate safely and efficiently, you need to understand an important principle of electronics called Ohm's law. It's actually a formula: the amount of resistance (in ohms) multiplied by the current (in amps) equals voltage (in volts). The measurements used in Ohm's law can be helpful in selecting the right parts, conducting path, and power source for a circuit.

Now imagine what it would be like to walk through a short, crowded hallway compared to a much longer crowded hallway. With more people in the long hallway you'd have a greater chance of bumping

THINGS ARE HEATING UP

For the circuits in computers, electric clocks, and other machines, keeping the temperature low is necessary. It can be dangerous for these circuits to get overheated. But if you want a piece of toast for breakfast, you want your toaster to get hot. The more resistance a circuit has, the more heat is created. For appliances such as toasters and heaters, resistors can actually create more heat by forcing electrons to move through thinner, longer wires.

You might notice that the cord of a cell phone charger gets warm after it's been charging for a while. Wires in this skinny cord have high resistance, meaning the electrons have less room to move.

into people. So there would be more resistance in a longer hallway. This is how Ohm's law applies to electrons colliding in a wire as well.

It's important to know the resistance in a circuit because resistance helps us control the flow of current. Too much current can heat up a wire or burn out a part, like the fan in a laptop computer. The less wiggle room electrons have in a conductor, the hotter things are going to get. All that bumping around creates friction, which means more heat.

That's why after it's been plugged in for a while, a skinny cell phone charger cord is more likely to feel warm to the touch than a thick extension cord. Thinner, longer wires mean greater resistance. Spreading out electrons in a thicker, shorter wire leads to less resistance and less heat.

CHAPTER TWO

DEVICES IN A CIRCUIT

If you look at any circuit, whether it's in a remote-controlled race car controller or in a computer, you'll see a mix of unusual-looking parts. Among the key parts, or components, of a circuit are resistors, capacitors, transistors, and LEDs.

RESISTORS

Controlling resistance usually involves more than choosing the right type of wire. Engineers have figured out how to design a circuit with the correct resistance by using a resistor. It helps the circuit keep a consistent amount of resistance and doesn't create too much or too little heat. A resistor also helps control the current running through the circuit. There are many different types of resistors.

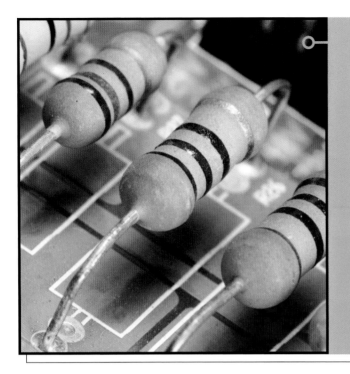

A computer circuit board requires many resistors to keep the computer's insides from burning out. Resistors can be made from several different materials, but many are made from carbon or a metal like copper. The resistors are the blue cylinders with the colored stripes. The colors and patterns help identify a resistor's value in ohms.

Choosing the right one depends on the size and purpose of the circuit.

CAPACITORS

The function of a circuit may also require that energy be stored temporarily until it is needed. A device called a capacitor stores electrical charge temporarily in two flat, rectangular pieces called plates—one positively charged and the other negatively charged. A capacitor looks and acts like a battery, but they are different in some important ways. A capacitor stores energy in an electrical field. A battery's energy comes from a chemical reaction inside the battery. Also, a battery can store more energy than a capacitor of similar size.

When more current is flowing in a circuit than there is demand for, a capacitor can store the extra charge. Then, when demand increases, capacitors can release the stored charge faster than a battery. That's because of the way a capacitor stores energy.

A battery stores its potential energy in a chemical form. A chemical reaction involving the zinc, chloride, nickel, or other chemicals in a battery must take place for electrical energy to be produced. This takes time. A camera's flash uses a capacitor because it needs energy for its light very quickly. Ever notice how the lights on a digital clock or your TV blink after you lose power in your home? That happens because the capacitor makes the lights blink the same way until the clock is reset. Think of a capacitor as a little storage tank full of energy, ready to release that power as soon as it's needed.

TRANSISTORS

A transistor can do two jobs. It can act as an amplifier, making a small current bigger when it exits the transistor. In a complicated circuit, one component, such as a resistor, may release a small amount of electric current. But another component, such as a lightbulb, may need a larger current to work. A transistor can make that happen. Transistors are also often used to amplify quiet sounds to become much louder. A transistor radio, for example, can receive radio signals through the air and change them to electrical signals that move through a transistor. Then the signals are amplified to come out of a speaker at whatever volume you want.

THE SMALLEST CIRCUITS

Microchips are little devices used to store memory and help a computer operate. Each microchip is a tiny circuit, with millions of microscopic resistors, capacitors, and transistors. A microchip is also called an integrated circuit, or IC.

ICs are used in computerized machines ranging from calculators to satellites. An IC differs from a regular circuit because it's made of semiconductor material—a substance that can transmit electrical energy only under certain circumstances.

You may not be able to see all the working parts of an IC, but if your computer is running smoothly, you know the IC is doing its job.

A transistor can be a switch too. It can use a smaller electric current to control a larger electric current. Transistors are very important components in most types of circuits. They can be tiny enough to be part of computer chips and big enough for use in larger circuits.

LEDs

Light-emitting diodes, or LEDs, are components that give off light. They're commonly used to let you know a circuit has power, like the tiny light that glows to tell you your computer is on.

These are just a few of the components used in circuits. There are also different types of circuits, each designed for a very specific job.

CHAPTER THREE

PARALLEL AND
SERIES CIRCUITS

Picture a simple circuit that includes a battery, three lightbulbs, and a wire that runs from the negative end of the battery. The wire goes from the battery to each of the three lightbulbs, connecting to the battery again at the positive end. That's an example of a series circuit. Every component in the circuit is connected in a group called a series, and only one wire, or conducting path, is present. With only one path, the entire current runs through each lightbulb, or load.

If that circuit is closed, all three bulbs will light. If there is an interruption of the current, they will all go out. That interruption might be a break in the wire, a broken lightbulb, or an open switch.

Imagine the lights in your home. You walk inside and flip a switch. If all the lights in your home were part of a series circuit, all the lights would go on when the switch is on. And they'd all go dark when the switch is turned off.

That doesn't sound like a great system for home lighting. You don't want lights on in rooms you're not

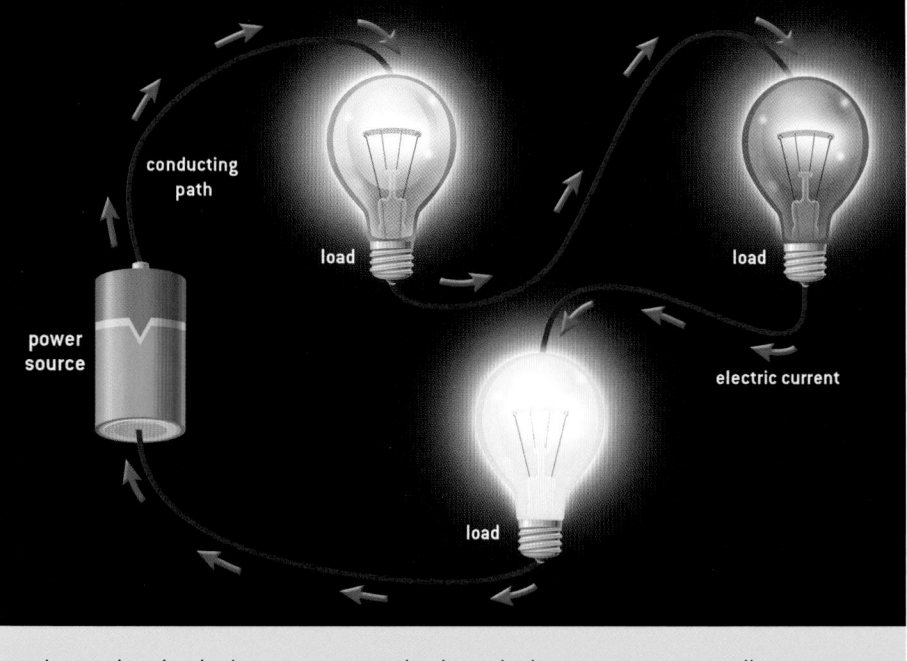

conducting path

load

load

power source

electric current

load

In a series circuit, the power source, loads, and other components are all connected by the same wire.

using. Or what if you only want your night-light on to read in bed? You wouldn't need a big overhead light too.

To prevent that very problem, the circuits that power homes and other buildings are parallel circuits. You may have learned in math class that parallel lines go in the same direction and are the same distance apart at all times. In electronics, a parallel circuit starts with a single conducting path, divides into two or more paths, and then comes back together in one path to finish the circuit. Parallel circuits are different from series circuits in a few ways, but the biggest is in how current flows through them.

Picture a very busy highway with several side streets branching off from the highway. Some cars will stay on the highway, while a few will go down each side street. If one of those side streets is blocked, that won't affect traffic on the highway or the other side streets.

In a parallel circuit, it's the same idea. The current will move along the main conducting path, but some of the energy will move down each side path to a different load. So in your home, you can have current running through your refrigerator but

PARALLEL CIRCUIT

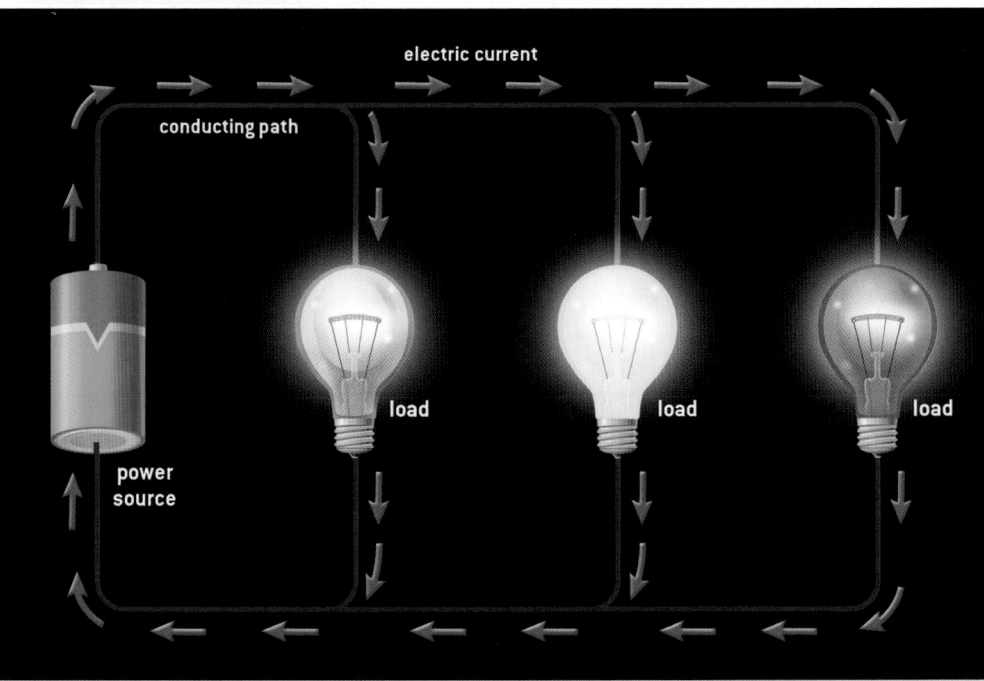

electric current

conducting path

load

load

load

power source

In a parallel circuit, the power source and certain components may be connected through a single wire but individual loads and other components may also branch off to a different wire before returning to the power source.

not to all the lights in the kitchen. A house or apartment building has one electrical line running to it from power lines that run aboveground or under the streets. Parallel circuits take that electricity and carry it throughout the house to power electronic devices. Unlike a series circuit, a parallel circuit will keep working if a bulb burns out or there's some other break in the flow of electrons. Holiday lights used to run on series circuits, so as soon as one bulb burned out, the whole string would go out. Someone could spend hours trying to find the one bulb that needed to be replaced.

It might seem like parallel circuits are better in every way, but a series circuit has advantages too. A series circuit needs less wiring. So for a simple circuit, like for switching a lamp on or off, a series design may be best. Also, a series circuit lets you know immediately if all the components are working or if one is broken. If all the parts of a series circuit are working, you'll know because

Have you ever seen a row of lightbulbs go out on a string of holiday lights? Modern lights are built with parallel circuits to avoid this problem.

there won't be an interruption of the electric current. If even one component in a series circuit is burned out, you'll know because nothing in the circuit will work.

POWER CHANGES

Another key difference between series and parallel circuits is how each one distributes power. Every component in a series circuit takes a little energy from the current. So if you have one series circuit with two lightbulbs and a second series circuit with the same current but with ten lightbulbs, the bulbs in the second series won't shine as brightly as the bulbs in the first circuit. That's because you're dividing the voltage among ten bulbs instead of just two. The more components added to a series circuit, the less power each component will have.

WHY IS IT CALLED A CIRCUIT?

When you draw a circle, you start at one point, make an o shape on your paper, and bring your pencil back to where you began. When your heart is pumping, blood leaves the heart and travels throughout your body to nourish your muscles and organs. Blood returns to the heart through your veins to start all over again. This is called circulation. The words *circle* and *circulation* are based on the ancient Latin word *circuitus*, meaning "going around." Since electric current in a circuit flows from one terminal at the power source all the way around to the other terminal, you can probably see why the word *circuit* makes sense.

A parallel circuit, however, provides the same amount of voltage to all parts of the circuit's load. This is because the current is split up evenly (if all loads are identical) to provide power to each component. It gets a little tricky when you have components that each require a different amount of resistance. But that's where resistors come in, to help make sure all elements in the circuit get just the right amount of current.

SOLVE IT!

HANGING HOLIDAY LIGHTS

During the holiday season, many families like to put up long strings of lights for decoration. Think about the lights you might hang from your roof, tree, or mantle. Should the lights run on a parallel or series circuit? Why? *(Answer key is on page 35.)*

CHAPTER FOUR

WHEN CIRCUITS
STOP CIRCULATING

Like any device, a circuit can stop working. Sometimes it's on purpose, as when you turn off the lights when leaving a room. But circuits can also become damaged or lose power unintentionally. Electricians call this a short circuit. A short circuit happens when too much current flows through the circuit, caused by the resistance in the circuit being too low. This might occur if the insulation around a wire wears out. The current traveling through the wire escapes and starts moving through another conducting path, such as a separate wire or a piece of metal.

A circuit may also stop working if two wires carrying electric current touch. If you've ever seen someone install an overhead light or a smoke detector or a ceiling fan, you may have noticed different colored wires—usually black, red, and white in the United States. The black wire is what's known as a hot wire, because it's carrying a current. It connects to the circuit breaker panel.

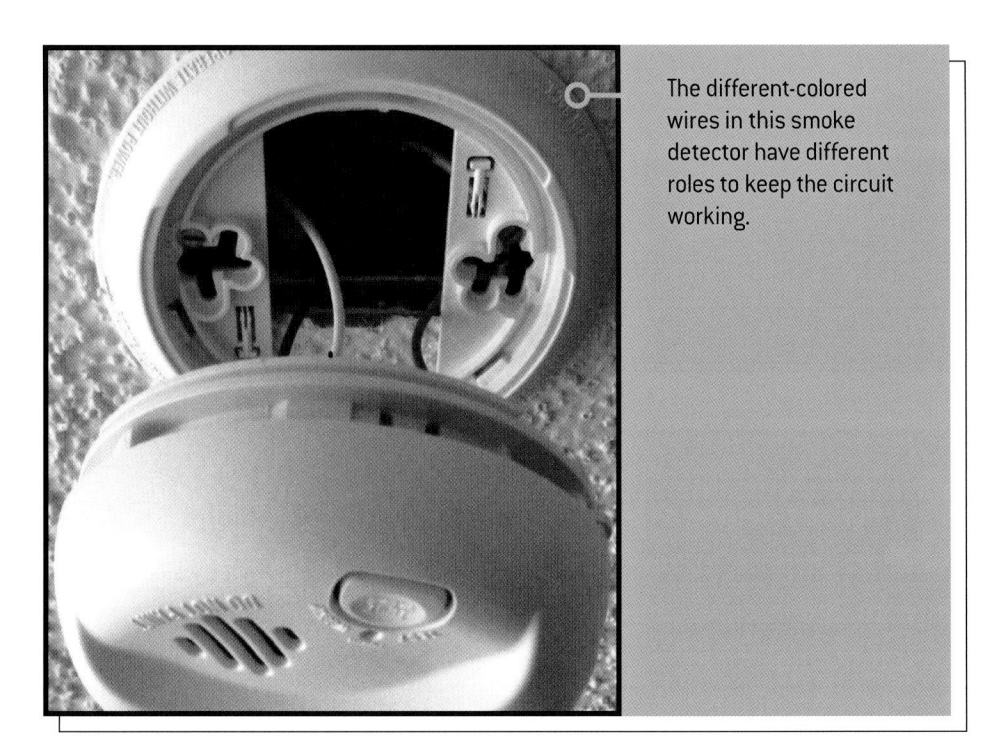
The different-colored wires in this smoke detector have different roles to keep the circuit working.

The white wire is known as a neutral or ground wire, and it helps to safely balance the voltage in the circuit. A short circuit can occur if a hot wire touches a neutral wire. The red wire is referred to as a secondary live wire because it can also carry a current in a 220-volt circuit, which is used in most houses.

Fortunately, large circuit systems, like those in your home, have ways of minimizing the harm of a short circuit.

CIRCUIT BREAKERS

As you've learned, controlling the current in any electrical system is important, both for safety and to help make sure the circuitry is working at its best.

But sometimes a current can get a little too large. A circuit gets overloaded when too much current runs through the circuit. For example, you might have a 15-amp circuit serving a room. But if you have 20 amps worth of electricity running through it because you have a lot of things plugged in and running at the same time, you could overload that circuit and trip the circuit breaker.

You may have seen the circuit breaker panel in your home. It usually just looks like a bunch of switches, but the circuit breaker is where electricity enters your home and is divided into separate circuits. Each of those switches are circuit breakers, and their job is to detect any dangerous changes in the current that could cause an overload or a short circuit. Each parallel circuit in the home has its own switch in the circuit breaker panel.

WHAT IS AN OPEN CIRCUIT?

When a circuit has a conducting path without any breaks from the negative end of a power source to the positive end, it's called a closed circuit. If there is any kind of break in the flow of electricity, that's called an open circuit, or an incomplete circuit. If a circuit breaker trips the circuit, the result is an open circuit. But if you turn an electrical device or a light switch to the Off position, you're also creating an open circuit. Removing a battery from a toy or device creates an incomplete circuit too.

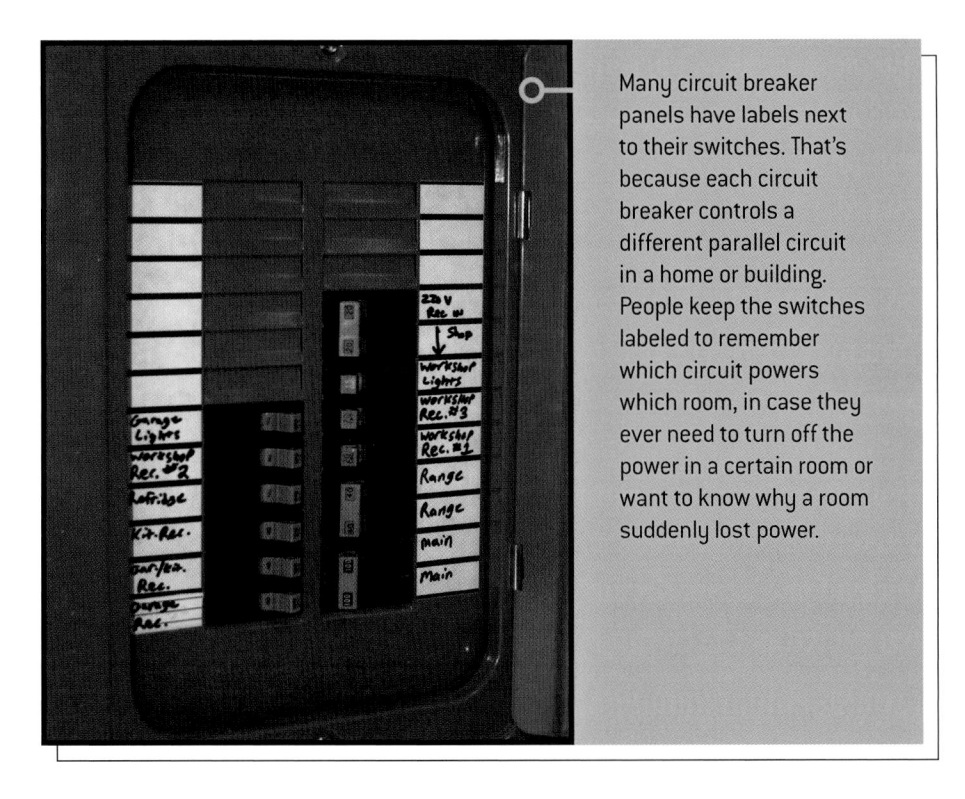

Many circuit breaker panels have labels next to their switches. That's because each circuit breaker controls a different parallel circuit in a home or building. People keep the switches labeled to remember which circuit powers which room, in case they ever need to turn off the power in a certain room or want to know why a room suddenly lost power.

A circuit breaker can help prevent an overloaded circuit from causing damage to electronics. If a circuit becomes overloaded, a circuit breaker should cut off power to the system. That's to help prevent a fire or other serious problems such as damage to your home's wiring or to appliances like your refrigerator or overhead lights.

Within each circuit breaker is an electromagnet that can operate a power switch. An electromagnet is a type of magnet that will attract or repel other objects only if an electric current is running through it. Without a current, there is no magnetic field.

When the current flow is normal, the magnet can't operate the switch that halts the current. But if the current gets too strong, the electromagnet can separate the two main parts of the switch to break the flow of electricity. This separation is known as tripping the circuit breaker.

If the problem is an overloaded circuit, turning off an appliance may be enough to allow you to reset the circuit breaker. If it's a short circuit and you try to reset it, the circuit breaker will trip again. And then it may be time to call an electrician.

SOLVE IT!

CHECKING THE CIRCUIT BREAKER

You're playing a video game while your brother practices his electric guitar and your sister dries her hair in the next room. A couple of lamps are on, and . . . oops! The power goes off in that part of your home. You and your parents check the circuit breaker, and you see that the breaker for that area has been tripped. What could be done to help restore power? *(Answer key is on page 35.)*

CHAPTER FIVE

AC AND DC

You've learned a lot about how an electric current flows in different types of circuits and how current can be restored if something breaks down. But did you know there are two kinds of electric currents? There's an alternating current (AC) and a direct current (DC). In direct current, electrons flow in one direction only and they can't be revved up to travel long distances. For a long time, DC was the primary source of power for homes and other buildings. But DC didn't always work well over a long distance. Newer technology that allows high-voltage DC to travel makes it work better for long distance use.

DC is an excellent choice for small components, such as transistors, though. Most electric toys and gadgets, such as remote-controlled cars, run on DC.

Most handheld electronics, like this tablet, run on direct current.

DIRECT CURRENT

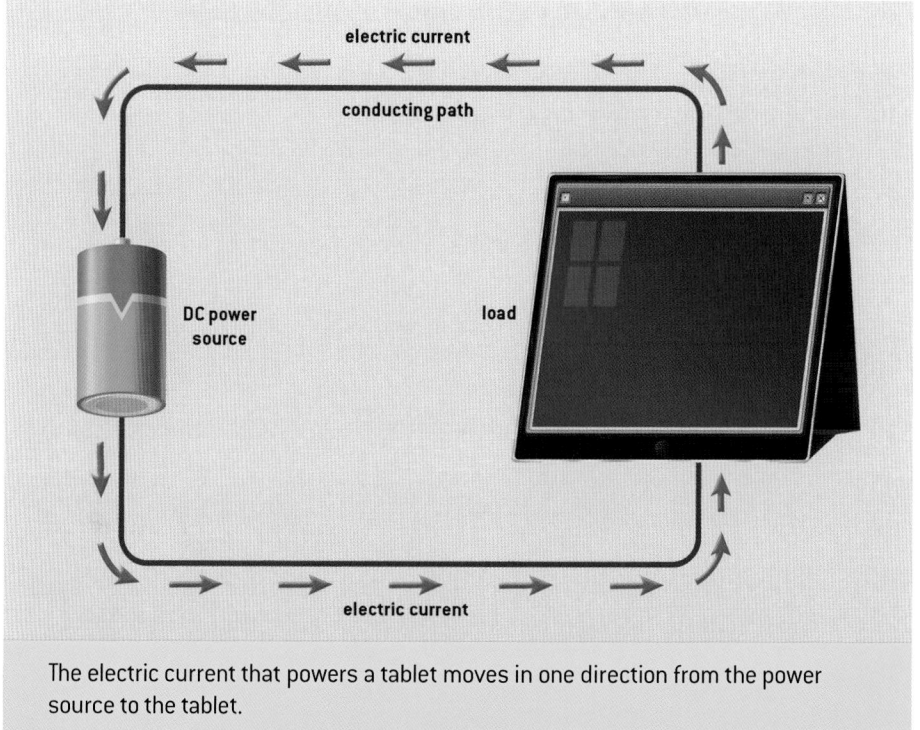

electric current

conducting path

DC power
source

load

electric current

The electric current that powers a tablet moves in one direction from the power source to the tablet.

AC is the better choice for currents that need to travel a long way from their source of power. In AC, electrons flow in one direction for a little while and then change direction for a little while before changing back.

The voltage in an alternating current can be increased, which makes it more powerful and better suited for long distance. So if a power plant is providing electricity for a town several miles away, it will need to use high voltage AC and transformers. A transformer is a device that can change the voltage passing

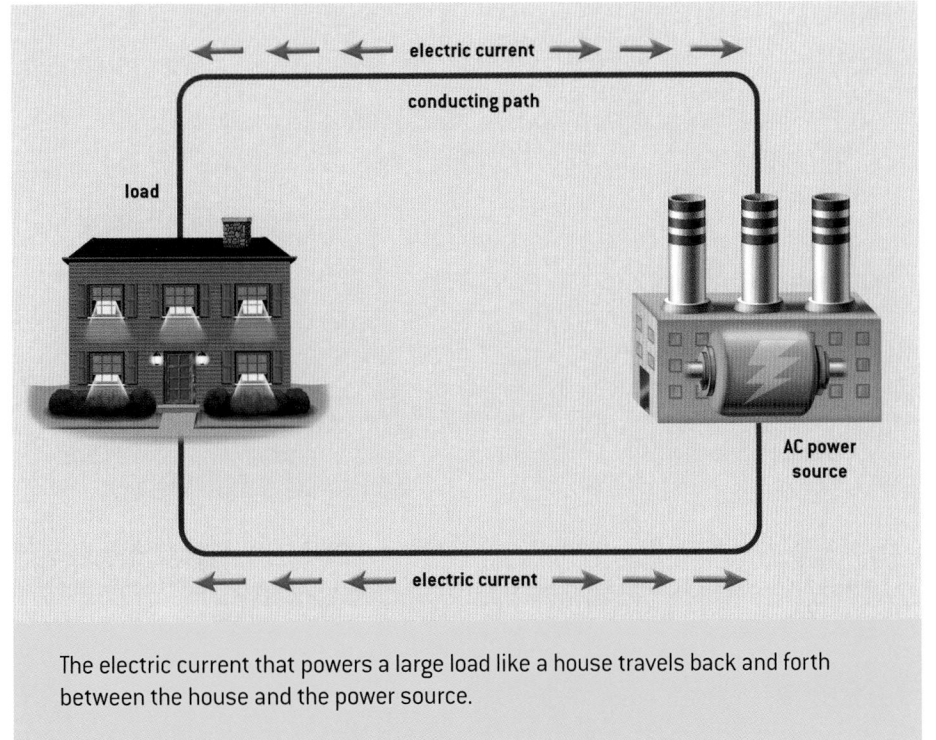

electric current

conducting path

load

AC power
source

electric current

The electric current that powers a large load like a house travels back and forth
between the house and the power source.

through it. Then the voltage can be lowered enough for a house
to use. Engineers call this stepping down the voltage. Without
transformers, all that high-voltage energy would fry the insulators
between the wires and circuits in your home.

The next time you look inside a computer or some other
complicated device, remember that all circuits work on a very
simple principle. You start with a power source, such as a battery or
a hydroelectric power plant, and you hook up the negative terminal
to a conducting path, such as a copper wire. Then you run that
path through transistors, capacitors, LEDs, video games, lights, or

CURRENT EVENTS WITH NIKOLA TESLA

Nikola Tesla (*right*) was born in 1856 in what is now Croatia and later moved to the United States. His greatest scientific achievements involved AC. Tesla developed the rotating magnetic field, the basis for much AC technology, where the opposite poles of the magnet circle around one point. The moving magnetic poles help change the direction electrons flow, which creates AC.

Tesla worked with George Westinghouse, an electrical engineer, in designing one of the world's first hydroelectric AC power plants, which produce energy using flowing or falling water. Tesla died in 1943, but his name and contributions continue to inspire scientists.

whatever else is in your circuit before you bring the path back to the positive end of your power source. Without interruptions, your circuit will keep the electricity flowing for a long time.

Power lines like this one carry alternating current across long distances.

MAKE YOUR OWN CIRCUIT

Using materials you can find in your home or school, you can make a simple circuit that will make a lightbulb glow.

WHAT YOU'LL NEED

- 2 8-inch (20-centimeter) by 2-inch (5 cm) strips of aluminum foil (without a plastic coating)
- 2 AA batteries
- electrical tape
- a lightbulb (an incandescent or compact fluorescent bulb will do)

WHAT YOU'LL DO

1. Roll two strips of aluminum foil into thin "wires."
2. Place the positive end of one battery against the negative end of the other. Wrap electrical tape around the connection to keep them touching.
3. Use electrical tape to attach one end of an aluminum foil wire to one of the battery terminals. Then do the same with the other wire and the other terminal.
4. Next, take a small lightbulb and attach the free end of one wire to the bottom of the bulb and the free end of the other wire to the threaded portion of the bulb.
5. Then see what happens.

FOLLOW-UP

What happens if you disconnect any one wire from the bulb or the battery? How might you connect a second lightbulb into this circuit?

HANGING HOLIDAY LIGHTS (PAGE 24)

Older holiday lights were made with series circuits, so if one bulb was burned out, the whole string of lights wouldn't work. Finally, manufacturers started making holiday lights with parallel circuits so one bad bulb wouldn't knock out the whole string.

CHECKING THE CIRCUIT BREAKER (PAGE 29)

This could be a case where you and your siblings overloaded the circuit that serves that part of the house. The circuit may have been designed to handle 15 amps, but you might have 20 amps of electricity running through the circuit to handle all those demands. Having your brother practice in a different part of the house and turning off a lamp or two might help. If you reduce the current demand on a circuit, you might be able to reset the circuit breaker and restore a safe and normal current.

GLOSSARY

amp: short for ampere, a unit of measure for electric current

circuit: a complete path an electric current travels to provide power to a component

component: any device or part of a circuit that affects the current

conductor: a substance through which electricity travels

electric current: in a circuit, the flow of electrons through a conductor

force: any action that produces, changes, or stops the shape or movement of an object

load: a component in a circuit that uses electric power

resistor: an electrical component that slows or reduces current in a circuit

terminal: the part of any component in a circuit that makes contact with the conducting path

transistor: a device that can amplify or switch electric signals

volt: a unit of measure for electric force in a circuit

SELECTED BIBLIOGRAPHY

"AC/DC: What's the Difference?" *American Experience. Accessed* December 16, 2015. http://www.pbs.org/wgbh/americanexperience/features/general-article/light-acdc.

Dahl, Øyvind Nydal. "Basic Electronic Components Used in Circuits." *Build Electronic Circuits.* May 13, 2013. http://www.build-electronic-circuits.com/basic-electronic -components.

"Nikola Tesla Biography." *Biography.* Accessed December 16, 2015. http://www .biography.com/people/nikola-tesla-9504443.

"What Are Amps, Watts, Volts and Ohms?" *How Stuff Works.* October 31, 2000. http://science.howstuffworks.com/environmental/energy/question501.htm.

Woodford, Chris. "Resistors." *Explain That Stuff.* Last modified August 6, 2015. http://www.explainthatstuff.com/resistors.html.

Circuit Builder

http://thefusebox.northernpowergrid.com/page/circuitbuilder.cfm

Visit this site to build your own circuits with different levels of difficulty.

Electric Play Dough

http://www.pbs.org/parents/adventures-in-learning/2014/02/electric-play-dough

Find out how everyday play dough can be used to help make a circuit.

Energy and Electricity Experiments

http://sciencewithkids.com/Experiments/Energy-Electricity-Experiments/energy
-experiments.html

Make lightbulb circuits, solar circuits, lemon and potato batteries, and more with the help of this hands-on set of easy, fun, and educational projects.

Fontichairo, Kristin, and AnnMarie P. Thomas. *Squishy Circuits*. Ann Arbor, MI: Cherry Lake, 2015.
Learn how to make circuits using clay and other unlikely materials in this short but fun take on circuitry and electronics.

Parker, Steve. *Electricity*. London: DK, 2013.
Discover the history of electricity, as well as the many fascinating uses of electricity.

Platt, Charles. *Make: Electronics*. 2nd ed. San Francisco: Maker Media, 2015.
This hands-on introduction to electronics encourages you to learn from your successes and your mistakes in building your own circuits.

Roland, James. *How LEDs Work*. Minneapolis: Lerner Publications, 2017.
Find out how these little lights use computer chip technology to brighten our world.

PHOTO ACKNOWLEDGMENTS

The images in this book are used with the permission of: © iStockphoto.com/da-vooda (electronic icon); © iStockphoto.com/Kubkoo (color dots background); © iStockphoto.com/alenaZ0509 (zigzag background); © iStockphoto.com/Sashatigar (robots and electrical microschemes); NASA, p. 4; © Blend Images/SuperStock, p. 7; Rob Schuster, pp. 8, 20, 21, 31, 32; © iStockphoto.com/restyler, p. 9; © Heritage Images/Hulton Archive/Getty Images, p. 10; © iStockphoto.com/Lawrence Sawyer, p. 11; © intararit/Shutterstock.com, p. 12; © Pictorial Press Ltd/Alamy, p. 13; © iStockphoto.com/veghsandor, p. 14; © iStockphoto.com/MarcoMarchi p. 16; © iStockphoto.com/kr7ysztof, p. 18; © iStockphoto.com/Jose Luis Gutierrez, p. 22; © Katy Warner/flickr.com (CC BY-SA 2.0), p. 26; © David Shwatal/Alamy, p. 27; © Doug Diamond/Alamy, p. 28; © iStockphoto.com/Marilyn Nieves, p. 30; Library of Congress (LC-DIG-ggbain-04851), p. 33 (top); © iStockphoto.com/DanBrandenburg, p. 33 (bottom).

Cover: © iStockphoto.com/connect11 (speakers); © iStockphoto.com/da-vooda (electronic icon); © iStockphoto.com/Kubkoo (color dots background); © iStockphoto.com/alenaZ0509 (zigzag background); © iStockphoto.com/Sashatigar (robots and electrical microschemes).